COUNCIL OF MILEUM

Synod of the African Church 416 AD

St. Aurelius
Archbishop of Carthage

Translated by: D.P. Curtin

COUNCIL OF MILEUM

Copyright @ 2022 Dalcassian Press

All rights reserved. No part of this publication may be reproduced, distributed, or transmitted in any form or by any means, including photocopying, recording, or other electronic or mechanical methods, without the prior written permission of the publisher, except in the case of brief quotations embodied in critical reviews and certain other non-commercial uses permitted by copyright law. For permission request, write to Dalcassian Press at dalcassianpublishing at gmail.com

ISBN: 979-8-8692-1013-5 (Paperback)

Library of Congress Control Number:
Author: Curtin, D.P. (1985-)

Printed by Ingram Content Group, 1 Ingram Blvd, La Vergne, Tennessee

First printing edition 2022.

COUNCIL OF MILEUM

TWO HUNDRED AND FOURTEENTH BISHOPS IN ATTENDANCE

TO THE MOST GLORIOUS EMPERORS ARCADIUS AND HONORIUS AUGUSTUS, FIVE TIMES CONSULS

SEPTEMBER 6TH.

In the city of Mileum, in the secretary of his own basilica, when Aurelius, bishop of the Church of Carthage, was sitting in a universal council, with the deacons present, Aurelius, the bishop, said: Since the body of the holy Church is one, and the head of all the members is one, it happened by the will of the Lord that we should come to this Church for the sake of love and brotherhood invited: whence I beseech your charity, because it is to be believed that our approach to you is neither superfluous nor inconvenient to all; and therefore also some of the causes of faith, from which the question of the Pelagians now looms, will be discussed first in this most holy group, and then some things which are necessary for ecclesiastical discipline will follow.

1. Against the Pelagians who say that Adam could have died even without sin.

Therefore it pleased all the bishops who were present in this holy synod to establish these things which were determined in the present council; that whoever says that Adam was made the first mortal man, so that whether he sinned or did not sin, he died in the body, that is, he came out of the body not by virtue of sin but by necessity of nature, let him be anathema.

II. According to the Apostle's testimony, even little ones who have not yet committed any sin are all truly baptized for the remission of sins.

Likewise, it was decided that whoever denies baptizing infants fresh from their mothers' wombs, or says that they are indeed baptized for the remission of sins, but derives nothing from Adam's original sin which is atoned for by the washing of regeneration, from which it follows that in them the form of baptism for the remission of sins is not indeed understood as true but false, let him be. For it is not otherwise to be understood what the Apostle says: Through one man sin entered into the world, and through sin death, and so death spread to all men in that they all sinned: except as the Catholic Church, diffused everywhere, has always understood. Because of this rule of faith, even little children, who have not yet been able to commit any sins in themselves, are therefore baptized in the remission of sins, so that what they have brought on by generation may be cleansed in them by regeneration.

III. That the grace of God not only forgives sins, but also helps them not to be committed.

Likewise, it was decided that anyone who says that the grace of God by which we are justified through Jesus Christ our Lord is valid only for the remission of sins that have already been committed, and not even for the helper so that they are not committed, should be anathema.

IV. That by the grace of God we know what we ought to do and love to do it.

Likewise, whoever says that the same grace of God through Jesus Christ our Lord helps us not to sin for this reason only, because by it the understanding of the commandments is revealed and opened to us, so that we may know what to desire and what we ought to avoid, but it is not provided to us through it that we know what to do also we must do it and be able to, let it be anathema. For when the apostle says: Knowledge inflates, but charity builds, it is very impious for us to believe that we have the grace of Christ for that which inflates, and for that which builds we have not, since both are the gift of God and to know what we ought to do and to love to do it, as a builder knowledge cannot be inflated by charity. But just as it is written about God: He teaches man knowledge, so it is also written: Charity is from God.

V. That the grace of God enables the law to be fulfilled, not, as Pelagius says, easily, as if without the grace of God it could be fulfilled with more difficulty.

Likewise, it was agreed that whoever says that the grace of justification is therefore given to us, so that what we are commanded to do by free will, we can fulfill more easily by grace, as if, even if grace were not given, it was not easy, but still we could fulfill the divine commands even without it, let him be anathema. For the Lord spoke of the fruits of the commandments when he did not say: Without me you can do more difficult things, but he said: Without me you can do nothing.

VI. According to the opinion of John the Evangelist, there is no one who can be without sin.

Likewise, it was agreed that what Saint John the Apostle said: If we say that we have no sin, we deceive ourselves and the truth is not in us. let it be. For the apostle continues and adds: But if we have confessed our sins, he is faithful and just who forgives us our sins and cleanses us from all unrighteousness: where it is sufficiently evident that this should be said not only humbly but also truthfully. For the Apostle could say: If we say that we have no sin, we exalt ourselves, and there is no humility in us; but when he says: We deceive ourselves, and the truth is not in us, he sufficiently shows that he who says he has no sin does not speak the truth but falsity.

VII. That each one must also speak justly, not only for others but for himself. Forgive us our debts.

Likewise, it was agreed that whoever should say: in the Lord's prayer should therefore say Saints, Forgive us our debts, that they should not say this for themselves, because that request is no longer necessary for them, but for others who are sinners among their people, and therefore not to say every one of the saints : forgive me my debts, but forgive us our debts, so that this may be understood as asking justly for others rather than for oneself, be anathema. For the apostle was holy and just, who said: For we all stumble in many things: for why was all added, except that this sentence might agree with the psalm where it is read: You shall not enter into judgment with your servant, for every living being shall not be justified in your sight: and in in the prayer of the most wise Solomon: There is not a man who will not sin against you: and in the book of holy Job: He signs in the hand of every man, that every man may know his infirmity: whence also the holy and just Daniel, when he said in prayer in the plural: We have sinned, we have done iniquity, and the rest which he confesses there truthfully and humbly, lest it should be thought, as some feel, that he did not say this about his sins but rather about his people's sins, after he said: when I prayed and confessed my sins and the sins of my people to my Lord God, he did not want to say our sins, but also he said to his people and to his own, because he foresaw the future of those who understood so badly as a prophet.

VIII. It is truly said by the saints: Forgive us our debts.

Also, it was decided that whoever uses the very words of the Sunday prayer where we say: Forgive us our debts, so the saints want it to be said so that this is not said humbly and truthfully, should be anathema. For who can make a man who prays, and lies not to men but to the Lord himself, who says with his lips that he wants to be forgiven, and says with his heart that he does not owe what is to be forgiven?

So far, the chapter on faith against the Pelagians. Now the ecclesiastical rules are discussed.

IX. That a general council ought to be assembled for the common causes of the Church: but for private causes the particular of each province. Also at first it was decided that there should be no need for an anniversary beyond tiring the brothers, but whenever a common cause demanded it, that is, of the whole of Africa, from wherever letters had been given to this seat for a council, that a synod should be assembled in that province where expediency had persuaded: but the causes which are not common they will be judged in their own provinces.

X. That the metropolitan signs and directs the letters to summon the council. It was also pleased at the request of all the bishops that your holiness alone subscribed to the letters to be given to all about the council.

XI. That whatever is established in the council concerning heretics or unbelievers may be demanded by the prince. It was pleased that the ambassadors sent by the glorious council against the heretics and heathens, or their superstitions, should obtain from the most glorious princes whatever they saw useful.

XII. That prayers or composed prayers, unless they have been approved by the council, should not be said. It was also agreed that prayers or prayers, or masses which had been approved in the council, or traditions or commendations or the laying on of hands, should be celebrated by all; perhaps something contrary to faith may have been composed either through ignorance or through interest.

XIII. That the latter should submit to the former bishops, and that they should not presume to do anything without consulting their primates.

Bishop Valentinus said: If the good of your patience permits, I will pursue those things which are necessary for ecclesiastical discipline. For we know that in this Church of Carthage the ecclesiastical discipline has always remained inviolable, so that no brother ever dared to put himself before his predecessors, but that was always presented to the predecessors by legitimate offices, which was always reasonably accepted by those who followed: may your holiness order that this order be better strengthened by your conversations. Aurelius, the bishop, said: It would not have been proper for us to repeat these things, unless there might have been some thoughtless minds which might have sharpened our senses to determine these things; but this is a common cause, which our brother and co-bishop insinuated, that each one of us should know the decree to such an extent that the latter should report to the former and not presume to do anything to the unconsulting primates. In this matter, those who thought that they should presume on something greater than the slanders, must be competently checked by the whole council. All the bishops said: This order was preserved both by the fathers and by the elders, and it will be preserved by us through the propitiation of God.

XIV. That the bishops should have letters from the ordinators for the time of their consecration.

Then it was decided that those who were subsequently ordained should receive letters from their ordainers signed by their own hands, containing the consul and the date, so that no dispute might arise about the latter or the former.

XV. So that wherever one reads first, the clerk should remain. Likewise, it was decided that anyone who read in the church for the first time or once was not bound to the clergy from another church.

XVI. That executors or advocates may be required by the prince for the causes of the churches.

Moreover, it was agreed that executors in all the desires of the church should be requested from the emperor, who should be imparted to each church. It was also agreed that the most illustrious emperors should be requested to order the judges to give the scholastic defenders requested to them, who are in the act or in the office of the defense of ecclesiastical causes, so that, after the manner of the priests of the province, the same who have undertaken the defense of the churches may have the capacity for the affairs of the churches, whenever necessity demands or to prevent stealthily, or to suggest the necessity, to enter the secretaries of the judges.

XVII. That neither the freed nor the freed be joined to the other.

It also pleased, according to the evangelical and apostolic discipline, that neither divorced from the wife, nor divorced from the husband, should be joined to another, but that they should remain so, or be reconciled to themselves. But if they have disdained, they must be reduced to penitence, in which case an imperial law is requested to be promulgated.

XVIII. Of those who do not communicate in their province and communicate elsewhere. It was decided that anyone who did not communicate in his own province sneaked into other provinces or overseas to communicate, to receive the loss of communion or clergy.

XIX. Of the clerics who implored a secular or synodal judgement. It was agreed that whoever requested from the emperor the knowledge of public judgments should be deprived of his own honor.

XX. That no one should go to the company without being trained, and how they should be trained.

It was decided that any cleric who, because of his necessity, wished to go somewhere to the congregation, should receive a formation from his bishop: he who wished to continue without formation, should be removed from communion. But if somewhere there arose a sudden necessity for him to go to the company, he should allege the very necessity to the bishop of his place, and he should convey the matter in writing to the same bishop. But the formations which are given by the primates or by any of the proper bishops should have the day of Easter; that if the day of Easter of the same year is still uncertain, the previous one should be added, as it is customary to write after the consulship in the public records.

XXI. Of the bishops who invaded the synod that they could repeat that which had been omitted.

Likewise, it was agreed that the bishops should not repeat any churches or peoples whom they think belong to their see, so that they act their cases before the bishops who judge them, but rush in with another restraint, whether unwilling or willing, the people suffer the loss of their cause: and whoever has already done this, if not yet the contention between the bishops is over, but they still contend that he should depart from thence whom he found to have rushed to the ecclesiastical judges; but whether he has the letter or not, let him meet the one who holds it and accept his letter, so that it may appear that he peacefully held the church belonging to him. But if he brings up any question, the cause shall be decided by the bishops as judges, either whom the primacy has given them, or whom the neighbors themselves have chosen in consultation with the primacy.

XXII. Of the clerics who complain of the judgments of their bishops.

Likewise, it was decided that priests, deacons, or other inferior clerics, in the cases they had, if they complained about the judgments of their bishops, the neighboring bishops should hear them, and whatever was between them should be used by them with the consent of their bishops. that even if they thought to be challenged by them, they would not challenge it except to the African councils or to the primates of their provinces; but those who thought to be appealed to overseas, should not be received for communion by anyone within Africa.

XXIII. Of those who have repented among the heretics, how they are to be received by the Church.

It was decided that anyone who had been converted by heretics and said that he had received penance from them, every Catholic bishop should inquire where and for what reason he had received penance from the same heretics, so that he could approve this very thing for himself with certain documents, according to the quality of the sin, as it seemed to the same Catholic bishop, a time He decides on repentance or reconciliation.

XXIV. Of the negligent bishops against the heretics.

Likewise, it was decided that whoever neglects to gain the places belonging to his see into Catholic unity, should be convened by the diligent neighboring bishops so that they do not hesitate to do so; that if they have not done so within six months from the date of the agreement, whoever was able to gain them should belong to him; so of course, that if he, to whom they seemed to have belonged, had been able to prove the negligence chosen by the heretics, that they should be there unpunished, and that his care had been anticipated, so that in this way he might avoid his care being more anxious, when the bishop's judges learned of this, they would restore the places of their seats. Of course, if the bishops between whom the case is contested are from different provinces, the primacy will appoint judges in whose province the place in question is contested; ; but it is not permitted to be challenged by the judges whom they have chosen by common consent: and whoever is proved by defiance unwilling to obey the judges, when this has been brought before the bishop of the first see, let him give a letter that none of the bishops shall communicate with him until he obeys.

XXV. Of which above

If a bishop has been negligent against heretics in the matrix of the chair, let him be summoned by the neighboring bishops who are careful, and his negligence will be shown to him so that he cannot excuse himself. that if, within six months from the day on which it is agreed, the execution takes place in his province, and he has not taken care to convert them to Catholic unity, it shall not be communicated to him until he fulfills it; he also loses his episcopate.

XXVI. Of virgins under the age of twenty-five who are covered by necessity.

Likewise it was decreed that anyone whose virginal chastity is endangered by the necessity of the bishops, when either a powerful suitor or a kidnapper is feared, or if she is in danger of death by a writ of penance, lest she die uncovered, or by demanding parents, or by those whose care it concerns, should veil the virgin within being in force five years of age, the council established for that number of years does not prevent him.

XXVII. Of the bishops who, after the proceedings of the Carthaginian synod, were retained to carry out the rest.

Likewise, it was decided that all the bishops who had assembled for the council should not be detained any longer, by the whole council three judges were chosen from each province: and they were chosen from the province of Carthage Vincentius, Fortunatianus and Clarus: from the province of Numidia Alipius, Augustine and Restitutus: from the province of Byzacena with St. Cresconius, Jucundus, and Aemilianus, the elder Donatian, in the primacy; they are already finished, or he himself signs the letters.

Aurelius, bishop of the Carthaginian church, signed.

Donatianus of Teleptensis subscribed to the first see.

Likewise all the bishops signed.

LATIN TEXT

CONCILIUM MILEVITANUM

DUCENTORUM QUATUORDECIM EPISCOPORUM AERA CCCCXL. GLORIOSISSIMIS IMPERATORIBUS ARCADIO QUINQUIES ET HONORIO AUGUSTO QUINQUIES CONSULIBUS

VI KALENDAS SEPTEMBRIS.

In civitate Milevitana in secretario basilicae ipsius cum Aurelius episcopus Ecclesiae Carthaginis in concilio universali consedisset, astantibus diaconibus, Aurelius episcopus dixit: Quoniam Ecclesiae sanctae unum est corpus, omniumque membrorum caput est unum, factum est volente Domino ut ad hanc Ecclesiam veniremus dilectionis et fraternitatis gratia invitati: unde quaeso charitatem vestram, quia ita credendum est quod noster accessus ad vos nec superfluus nec insuavis est cunctis; ideoque pariter quaedam de causis fidei, unde nunc quaestio Pelagianorum imminet, in hoc coetu sanctissimo primitus tractentur, deinde subsequantur et aliqua quae disciplinae ecclesiasticae necessaria existunt.

I. Contra Pelagianos qui dicunt etiam sine peccato mori potuisse Adam.

Placuit igitur omnibus episcopis, qui fuerunt in hac sancta synodo, constituere haec quae in praesenti concilio definita sunt; ut quicunque dicit Adam primum hominem mortalem factum, ita ut sive peccaret sive non peccaret moreretur in corpore, hoc est de corpore exiret non peccati merito sed necessitate naturae, anathema sit.

II. Quod juxta Apostoli testimonium etiam parvuli qui nihil peccati adhuc commiserunt omnes in peccatorum remissionem veraciter baptizentur.

Item placuit, ut quicunque parvulos recentes ab uteris matrum baptizandos negat aut dicit in remissionem quidem peccatorum eos baptizari, sed nihil ex Adam trahere originalis peccati quod lavacro regenerationis expietur, unde fit consequens ut in eis forma baptismatis in remissionem quidem peccatorum non vera sed falsa intelligatur, anathema sit. Quoniam non aliter intelligendum est quod ait Apostolus: Per unum hominem peccatum intravit in mundum et per peccatum mors, et ita in omnes homines mors pertransiit in quo omnes peccaverunt: nisi quemadmodum Ecclesia catholica ubique diffusa semper intellexit. Propter hanc enim regulam fidei etiam parvuli, qui nihil peccatorum in semetipsis adhuc committere potuerunt, ideo in peccatorum remissionem baptizantur, ut in eis regeneratione mundetur quod generatione traxerunt.

III. Quod gratia Dei non solum peccata dimittat, sed etiam adjuvet ne committantur.

Item placuit, ut quicunque dixerit gratiam Dei qua justificamur per Jesum Christum Dominum nostrum ad solam remissionem peccatorum valere quae jam commissa sunt, non etiam ad adjutorium ut non committantur, anathema sit.

IV. Quod per gratiam Dei sciamus quid facere debeamus et diligere ut faciamus.

Item quisquis dixerit eamdem gratiam Dei per Jesum Christum Dominum nostrum propter hoc tantum nos adjuvare ad non peccandum, quia per ipsam nobis revelatur et aperitur intelligentia mandatorum, ut sciamus quid appetere, quid vitare debeamus, non per illam autem nobis praestari ut quod faciendum cognoverimus etiam facere debeamus atque valeamus, anathema sit. Cum enim dicat Apostolus: Scientia inflat, charitas vero aedificat, valde impium est ut credamus ad eam quae inflat nos habere gratiam Christi et ad eam quae aedificat non habere, cum sit utrumque donum Dei et scire quid facere debeamus et diligere ut faciamus, ut aedificante charitate scientia non possit inflare. Sicut autem de Deo scriptum est: Qui docet hominem scientiam, ita etiam scriptum est: Charitas ex Deo est.

V. Quod gratia Dei praestet ut lex impleatur, non sicut ait Pelagius facile, quasi sine gratia Dei difficilius possit impleri.

Item placuit, ut quicunque dixerit ideo nobis gratiam justificationis dari, ut quod facere per liberum jubemur arbitrium facilius possimus implere per gratiam, tanquam, etsi gratia non daretur, non quidem facile, sed tamen possemus etiam sine illa implere divina mandata, anathema sit. De fructibus enim mandatorum Dominus loquebatur ubi non ait: Sine me difficilius potestis facere, sed ait: Sine me nihil potestis facere.

VI. Quod juxta sententiam Joannis evangelistae nemo sit qui esse possit sine peccato.

Item placuit, ut quod ait sanctus Joannes apostolus: Si dixerimus quia peccatum non habemus, nos ipsos decipimus et veritas in nobis non est, quisquis sic accipiendum putaverit, ut dicat propter humilitatem non oportere dici nos non habere peccatum, non quia veritas est, anathema sit. Sequitur enim Apostolus et adjungit: Si autem confessi fuerimus peccata nostra, fidelis est et justus qui remittat nobis peccata et mundet nos ab omni iniquitate: ubi satis apparet hoc non tantum humiliter sed etiam veraciter dici. Poterat enim apostolus dicere: Si dixerimus quia non habeamus peccatum, nos ipsos extollimus et humilitas in nobis non est; sed cum ait: Nos ipsos decipimus et veritas in nobis non est, satis ostendit eum qui dixerit se non habere peccatum non verum loqui sed falsum.

VII. Quod unicuique etiam justo non solum pro aliis sed pro semetipso dicere oporteat. Dimitte nobis debita nostra.

Item placuit, ut quicunque dixerit: in oratione dominica ideo dicere sanctos Dimitte nobis debita nostra, ut non pro se ipsis hoc dicant, quia non eis jam necessaria ista petitio, sed pro aliis qui sunt in suo populo peccatores, et ideo non dicere unumquemque sanctorum: dimitte mihi debita mea, sed dimitte nobis debita nostra, ut hoc pro aliis potius quam pro se justus petere intelligatur, anathema sit. Sanctus enim et justus erat apostolus qui dicebat: In multis enim offendimus omnes: nam quare additum est omnes, nisi ut ista sententia conveniret et psalmo ubi legitur: Non intres in judicium cum servo tuo, quoniam non justificabitur in conspectu tuo omnis vivens: et in oratione sapientissimi Salomonis: Non est homo qui non peccet tibi: et in libro sancti Job: In manu omnis hominis signat, ut sciat omnis homo infirmitatem suam: unde etiam Daniel sanctus et justus cum in oratione pluraliter diceret: Peccavimus, iniquitatem fecimus, et caetera quae ibi veraciter et humiliter confitetur, ne putaretur, quemadmodum quidam sentiunt, hoc non de suis sed de populi sui potius dixisse peccatis, posteaquam dixit: cum orarem et confiterer peccata mea et peccata populi mei domino Deo meo, noluit dicere peccata nostra, sed et populi sui dixit et sua, quoniam futuros istos qui tam male intelligerent tanquam propheta praevidit.

VIII. Quod a sanctis veraciter dicatur: Dimitte nobis debita nostra.

Item placuit, ut quicunque verba ipsa dominicae orationis ubi dicimus: Dimitte nobis debita nostra, ita volunt a sanctis dici ut humiliter non veraciter hoc dicatur, anathema sit. Quis enim ferat orantem, et non hominibus sed ipsi Domino mentientem, qui labiis sibi dicit dimitti velle, et corde dicit quae sibi dimittantur se debita non habere?

Hucusque de fide capitula contra Pelagianos. Nunc regulae tractantur ecclesiasticae.

IX. Ut in communes causas Ecclesiae generale concilium congregari oporteat: in privatis vero causis speciale uniuscujusque provinciae. Item primitus placuit, ut non sit ultra fatigandis fratribus anniversaria necessitas, sed quoties exegerit causa communis, id est totius Africae, undecunque ad hanc sedem pro concilio datae litterae fuerint, congregandam esse synodum in ea provincia ubi opportunitas persuaserit: causae autem quae communes non sunt in suis provinciis judicentur.

X. Ut epistolas ad concilium devocandum metropolitanus subscribat et dirigat.

Placuit etiam petitu omnium episcoporum, ut epistolis omnibus de concilio dandis sanctitas tua sola subscribat.

XI. Ut de haereticis vel infidelibus quidquid in concilio constituitur a principe impetretur. Placuit, ut et illud adversus haereticos et Paganos vel eorum superstitiones legati missi de hoc a glorioso concilio, quidquid utile praeviderint, de gloriosissimis principibus impetrent.

XII. Ut preces vel orationes compositae, nisi probatae fuerint in concilio, non dicantur. Placuit etiam et illud, ut preces vel orationes, seu missae quae probatae fuerint in concilio, seu traditiones sive commendationes seu manus impositiones ab omnibus celebrentur: nec aliqua ex his omnino dicantur in Ecclesia, nisi quae a prudentioribus tractata et comprobata in synodo fuerint, ne forte aliquid contra fidem vel per ignorantiam vel per studium sit compositum.

XIII. Ut posteriores anterioribus episcopis deferant, nec inconsultis primatibus suis aliquid agere praesumant.

Valentinus episcopus dixit: Si permittit bonum patientiae vestrae, prosequor ea quae necessaria sunt ecclesiasticae disciplinae. Scimus enim in hac Ecclesia Carthaginensi inviolate semper permansisse ecclesiasticam disciplinam, ita ut nullus fratrum prioribus suis se aliquando auderet anteponere, sed officiis legitimis id semper exhibitum est prioribus, quod ab insequentibus rationabiliter semper acciperetur: hunc ordinem jubeat sanctitas vestra melius vestris interlocutionibus roborari. Aurelius episcopus dixit: Non decuerat quidem ut haec repeteremus, nisi forte existerent inconsideratae mentes quorumdam quae ad haec statuenda nostros acuerent sensus; sed communis haec causa est quam insinuavit frater et coepiscopus noster, ut unusquisque nostrum sibi decretum adeo cognoscat, ut posteriores anterioribus deferant nec inconsultis primatibus aliquid agere praesumant. Qua de re oportet eos qui putaverint spretis majoribus aliquid praesumendum, competenter esse ab omni concilio coercendos. Universi episcopi dixerunt: Hic ordo et a patribus et a majoribus servatus est, et a nobis Deo propitio servabitur.

XIV. Ut episcopi pro tempore consecrationis suae litteras ab ordinatoribus habeant.

Deinde placuit, ut quicunque deinceps ordinantur litteras accipiant ab ordinatoribus suis manu eorum subscriptas, continentes consulem et diem, ut nulla altercatio de posterioribus vel anterioribus oriatur.

XV. Ut ubi quis primum legerit, ibi permaneat clericus. Item placuit, ut quicunque in ecclesia primum vel semel legerit ab alia ecclesia ad clericatum non teneatur.

XVI. Ut pro causis ecclesiarum exsecutores vel advocati a principe postulentur.

Placuit praeterea, ut exsecutores in omnibus desideriis quae habet ecclesia ab imperatore postulentur, qui singulis ecclesiis impertiantur. Placuit etiam, ut petatur a gloriosissimis imperatoribus ut jubeant judicibus dare petitos sibi defensores scholasticos, qui in actu sint vel in officio defensionum causarum ecclesiasticarum, ut more sacerdotum provinciae idem ipsi qui defensionem ecclesiarum susceperint habeant facultatem pro negotiis ecclesiarum, quoties necessitas flagitaverit vel ad obsistendum obrepentibus, vel ad necessaria suggerenda, ingredi judicum secretaria.

XVII. Ut neque dimissus neque dimissa alteri conjungantur.

Placuit quoque secundum evangelicam et apostolicam disciplinam, ut neque dimissus ab uxore, neque dimissa a marito, alteri conjungatur, sed ita maneant, aut sibimet reconcilientur. Quod si contempserint, ad poenitentiam redigantur, in qua causa legem imperialem petendam promulgari.

XVIII. De his qui in sua provincia non communicant et alibi communicant. Placuit, ut quicunque non communicans in propria provincia in aliis provinciis vel in transmarinis partibus ad communicandum obrepserit, jacturam communionis vel clericatus excipiat.

XIX. De clericis qui apud principem saeculare judicium aut synodale imploraverint. Placuit, ut quicunque ab imperatore cognitionem publicorum judiciorum petierit honore proprio privetur: si autem episcopale judicium ab imperatore postulaverit, nihil ei obsit.

XX. Ut sine formatis nemo ad comitatum proficiscatur, et qualiter fiant formatae.

Placuit, ut quicunque clericus propter necessitatem suam alicubi ad comitatum ire voluerit, formatam (0233C)ab episcopo suo accipiat: qui sine formata voluerit pergere, a communione removeatur. Quod si alicubi ei repentina necessitas orta fuerit ad comitatum pergendi, alleget apud episcopum loci ejus ipsam necessitatem, et de hoc rescripta ejusdem episcopi perferat. Formatae autem quae a primatibus vel a quibusque episcopis propriis dantur habeant diem paschae; quod si adhuc ejusdem anni paschae dies incertus est, ille praecedens adjungatur, quomodo solet post consulatum in publicis gestis ascribi.

XXI. De episcopis qui id quod repetere poterant praetermissa synodo invaserint.

Item placuit, ut episcopi quascunque ecclesias vel plebes quas ad suam cathedram existimant pertinere non ita repetierint, ut causas suas episcopis judicantibus agant, sed alio retinente irruerint, sive nolentibus sive volentibus plebibus, causae suae detrimentum patiantur: et quicunque hoc jam fecerunt, si nondum est inter episcopos finita contentio, sed adhuc inde contendunt, ille inde discedat quem constiterit praetermissis judicibus ecclesiasticis irruisse: nec sibi quisque blandiatur, si a primatu ut retineat litteras impetrarit; sed sive habeat litteras, sive non habeat, conveniat eum qui tenet et ejus litteras accipiat, ut appareat pacifice tenuisse ecclesiam ad se pertinentem. Si autem ille aliquam quaestionem retulerit, per episcopos judices causa finiatur, sive quos eis primatus dederit, sive quos ipsi vicinos cum consultu primatis delegerint.

XXII. De clericis qui de judiciis episcoporum suorum conqueruntur. Item placuit, ut presbyteri, diaconi vel caeteri inferiores clerici, in causis quas habuerint, si de judiciis episcoporum suorum questi fuerint, vicini episcopi eos audiant, et inter eos quidquid est finiant adhibiti ab eis ex consensu episcoporum suorum; quod si et ab eis provocandum putaverint, non provocent nisi ad Africana concilia vel ad primatus provinciarum suarum: ad transmarina autem qui putaverint appellandum, a nullo intra Africam ad communionem suscipiantur.

XXIII. De his qui apud haereticos poenitentiam acceperunt quomodo ab Ecclesia recipiantur.

Placuit, ut quicunque conversus ab haereticis dixerit se apud eos poenitentiam accepisse, unusquisque catholicus episcopus requirat ubi et ob quam causam apud eosdem haereticos poenitentiam susceperit, ut cum certis documentis hoc ipsum sibi approbaverit, pro qualitate peccati, sicut eidem episcopo catholico visum fuerit, tempus poenitentiae vel reconciliationis decernat.

XXIV. De episcopis negligentibus adversus haereticos.

Item placuit, ut quicunque negligunt loca ad suam cathedram pertinentia in catholicam unitatem lucrari, conveniantur a diligentibus vicinis episcopis ut id agere non morentur; quod si intra sex menses a die conventionis non effecerint, qui potuerit lucrari ea ad ipsum pertineant; ita sane, ut si ille, ad quem pertinuisse videbantur, probare potuerit magis illius electam negligentiam ab haereticis ut impune ibi sint, et suam diligentiam fuisse praeventam ut eo modo ejus cura sollicitior vitaretur, cum hoc judices episcopi cognoverint, suae cathedrae loca restituant. Sane si episcopi inter quos causa versatur diversarum sunt provinciarum, ille primatus det judices, in cujus provincia est locus de quo contenditur: si autem ex communi placito vicinos judices elegerint, aut unus eligatur aut tres, ut si tres elegerint aut omnium sententiam sequatur aut duorum; a judicibus autem quos communis consensus elegerit non liceat provocare: et quisquis probatus fuerit per contumaciam nolle obtemperare judicibus, cum hoc primae sedis episcopo fuerit prolatum, det litteras ut nullus ei communicet episcoporum donec obtemperet.

XXV. De quibus supra.

Si in matricibus cathedris episcopus negligens fuerit adversus haereticos, conveniatur a vicinis episcopis diligentibus, et ei sua negligentia demonstretur ut se excusare non possit; quod si ex die quo convenitur intra sex menses in ejus provincia exsecutio fuerit, et non eos ad unitatem catholicam convertendos curaverit, non ei communicetur donec impleat: si autem probatum fuerit eum de communione illorum fuisse mentitum, dicendo eos communicasse quos eo sciente non communicasse constiterit, etiam episcopatum amittat.

XXVI. De virginibus quae infra viginti quinque annos necessitate cogente velantur.

Item placuit, ut quicunque episcoporum necessitate periclitantis pudicitiae virginalis, cum vel petitor potens vel raptor aliquis formidatur, vel si etiam aliquo in mortis periculo scripulo compuncta fuerit, ne non velata moriatur, aut exigentibus parentibus, aut his ad quorum curam pertinet, velaverit virginem intra vigenti quinque annos aetatis, non ei obsit concilium quod de isto numero annorum constitutum est.

XXVII. De episcopis qui post acta Carthaginensi synodo retenti sunt ad reliqua peragenda.

Item placuit, ne diutius universi episcopi qui ad concilium congregati sunt tenerentur, ab universo concilio judices ternos de singulis provinciis eligi: et electi sunt de provincia Carthaginensi Vincentius, Fortunatianus et Clarus: de provincia Numidiae Alipius, Augustinus et Restitutus: de provincia Byzacena cum sancto sene Donatiano primatu Cresconius, Jucundus et Aemilianus: de Mauritania Sitiphensi Severianus, Casiatticus et Donatus: de provincia Tripolitana Plautius, qui ex more legatus unus est missus: qui omnes cum sancto sene Aurelio universa cognoscant, a quo petiit universum concilium ut cunctis sive gestis quae confecta jam sunt seu epistolis ipse subscribat.

Aurelius episcopus ecclesiae Carthaginensis subscripsit.

Donatianus Teleptensis primae sedis subscripsit.

Similiter et omnes episcopi subscripserunt.

The Scriptorium Project is the work of a small group of lay people of various apostolic churches who are interested in the preservation, transmission, and translation of the works of the early and medieval church. Our efforts are to make the works of the church fathers accessible to anyone who might have an interest in Christian antiquities and the theological, philosophical, and moral writings that have become the bedrock of Western Civilization.

To-date, our releases have pulled from the Greek, Syriac, Georgian, Latin, Celtic, Ethiopian, and Coptic traditions of Christianity, and have been pulled from sundry local traditions and languages.

Other Catalogue Titles for the Early Punic Church in North Africa:

Seven Rules by Ticonius the Donatist *(July 2006)*
Letters on the Council of Ephesus by Capreolus of Carthage (Aug. 2007)
The Time of the Barbarians by St. Quoddeusvult of Carthage (Feb. 2009)
Two Letters from Byzantine Africa by Licinianus of Carthage (Oct. 2016)
Apology to Gunthamund, King of Vandals by Blossius Aemilius Dracontius (Feb. 2018)
Letter to Pope Theodore by Victor of Carthage (Feb. 2020)
Council of Mileum by St. Aurelius of Carthage (Aug. 2022)
Against Palladius the Arian by Vigilius of Thapsus (Nov. 2023)
Response Against Arians by St. Fulgentius of Ruspe (Jan. 2024)
The Final Letter to Latin North Africa by Pope Leo IX (Mar. 2024)
Letters & Pamphlets by Fulgentius Ferrandus (Apr. 2024)